First printing edition 2024.

ISBN: 978-1-962891-05-9 (eBook)
ISBN: 978-1-962891-21-9 (Paperback)

unfinished
Published by Vellichor and More
https://jessicapietroart.wixsite.com/1234/

unfinished

jessica pietro

Vellichor and More

For Vincent.
My first miracle.
The sweetest of the sunflowers.
You may not yet understand all the words within these pages,
but I hope you grow up knowing how great of an impact
your existence had on my story and that
I thank God for you every single day.

Because He loves you.
Because He wants you to grow.
Because He wants to use you.
Because He wants you to know your
pain was for a purpose.

one

A tear slides down my cheek, and I swipe it away.
    My skin is hot with rage and pain.
    The carpet is scratchy beneath me.
    I hear them at my back,

                    whispering.

    Shifting on the couch.

        I
             know
                 what
                      they're
                            doing.

A light buzzes in the reptile tank,
    so faint it's like a ringing in my ears.

They ask me to join them.
    I think saying *no* will reveal how upset this makes me.

I think laying with my back to them will make them see.

He is mine. She is my friend.

A week later, I pretend nothing is wrong.
    A habit of mine.
    Hiding agony behind thick scales.

In this case, actual scales, as I do a sexy dance on his friend with a snake draped over my shoulders—full on Brittney style.

He is furious.
    How? How can he be after what he did?
    I thought he was different.
    Don't I always?

Okay, not *always*.
    Sometimes I see right into their vile soul, and still, I

                dangle   flaunt   tease.

    The need to feel wanted is like a fire in me craving oxygen.

Anyway.
    I thought he was different. He saved me from the other one.
    My savior. Pulled me from the darkness.
    Convinced me that I *deserved* better.
    A lie, but everything in me longed to believe it.

Later, we end things. But it's always tricky in a group of friends.
    Though they were his friends first,
                I am still invited.

I kill at pong.
    He ignores me.

I dance to the music. It's freezing in this garage,
        even with the fire and the booze.
                He ignores me.

I flirt with his friends.
    He ignores me. Until he doesn't.

I turn him down. I thought I deserved better?

Sweet pills up my nose always make me black out.
    I never black out, except on these babies.
    Tiny little sugar delights go up easy with little
    residue or clogging.
    It doesn't take much to be

        free
                flying
                        gone.

He doesn't know. No one does.
    I've been hiding it. From everyone.
    It's the only thing that smothers the darkness.

And when this prescription runs out, it will be a while
        until I can get more. Can't risk them being
                flushed by a couple of do-gooders.
        Can't be making anyone worry, especially here.
                They don't do that kind of thing here.

Still, he must know I'm wasted, right?
    Hear the slur in my words.
    See the   w o b b l e   in my steps.
    I guess he's wasted, too.

I remember his hands on me. I remember pushing him away.
    I wake up the next morning in his bed with
        wetness between my legs.

Then I throw up.
    Luckily…I manage to crawl over him and reach the toilet.

Darkness swallows me up. Clinging to me like sludge,
        like Venom.
    I make my way to the kitchen for a shot of tequila
        to fight
            the cold
                outside

                        and in my heart.
   Then I grab my keys,
      and I never go back there again.

I thought I deserved better?

    Who am I kidding? I never really believed that anyway.

At the end of this book is a curated playlist of songs. One for each chapter.

two

He wasn't the only creep to send me on this spiral.
There were many others. Long before him.

I can still feel them standing behind me,
hands on my tiny shoulders.
Man hands.
Rough and thick and sickening.

Why do men always do that?
They think it's a comfort?
They think shoulders are a safe place to touch?
Somewhere a father might offer kindness.

Security.

Old men always like me.
I never understood why.
Perhaps I was prettier when I was younger.
When I grew up, I had to practically
throw myself
at men my age to glean attention.

Show a little skin, flirt, dance.

But at thirteen, I'm a doll. Precious. A prize to be cherished.

Even standing next to an adult woman,
        gorgeous blond curls flowing to the center of her back
                and hips that fill her swimsuit to perfection,
                                        they look at me.

They ask if I'm a model, too.

I blush, not to be coy, but because
        compliments make me uncomfortable
                —especially when they come from old men.

That's what men do. They make you uncomfortable.

Of course I'm not a model. I'm a child.
                No bosom yet to speak of.
        The tiniest of hills barely visible through my shirt.
        Lots of big boobs on display all around you. In swimsuits.
                So why are you looking at me?

As girls, we learn to be polite.
        If I had a girl, I'd teach her to defend herself against
                        men like that.
        Punch them right between the legs.
        So when they look at you later,

                their man parts hurt instead of harden.

I'm not usually violent, and I never want to teach that violence is the answer, but there are too many old bastards out there preying on young girls.

A line has to be drawn, and if I could do it all over again,

                  I'd choose violence from day one.

I never do, of course. Not once.
    I just give in.
    Polite.
    Tears in my eyes until it's over.

I want to be liked, right?
        I want to be special?
                So I have to give them what they want.

Men are stupid.

        So are friends.

         So are people.

three

I don't have a girl.
   I have a boy. At 19.
   What a life.

His sperm donor breaks me into pieces. Shatters me.
   Over and over and over.
            Why do I let him? Why do I keep coming back?
   Why do I put up with
               insanity and abuse?
                              I guess I'm used to it.

Raised by a master manipulator.
   Narcissistic and horrible.
                  Also awesome.
                     And caring... It's confusing.

Moving on...
   I don't deserve better. That's why I stay.
   My saviornotasavior is wrong.
            And let's be honest here,
                     c a r d s   o n   t h e   t a b l e :

I am insane, too.
        Broken.
                Erratic.

I try to control him so he won't hurt me anymore.
    And in truth, I hit him first.
        He told me to.
    So I punched him square in the jaw.
    I suppose I did choose violence,
                    just this once.

But *he told me to.*
    I guess he didn't think I would.

It was downhill from there.
    To this day, I can't remember if we got along before that.
        It was pretty early on.
    We were only half fighting when it happened.
        And drunk.
                Maybe it was my fault all along.

When he sleeps with my friend
        in our house
            as our son lays next to me
            in our room,

I finally leave him… (for the tenth time).

I leave a note that says,

        You broke my heart, I broke your guitar.

    Dramatic, I know.

He wasn't any good anyway.
    At guitar, I mean.
    Well, at anything, really.
            Still, I take him back.

Once, I said to a friend,
                One day I'll be strong enough to leave him.

I sit in my car, clutching my infant,
            tears streaming down my face.
                    He bangs on the windows. Dents the door.
    Screaming at the top of his lungs.
                        Yukon always makes him rage.

I forgot the keys. I'm trapped.
    With an infant.

Does my son have any hope after all he's been through from the
moment he arrived in this messed up world?

Even that isn't enough.
    He lures me back with promises
            I   k n o w   h e   w o n ' t   k e e p .
    But we have a son.
            He needs his father.

And I'm terrified to be alone.

At last, I leave him for good.
    Our son is 6 months old.
    I worry he'll hit him, too.
            So I leave.   Or he leaves.

Who really knows anymore who's making these decisions.

Regardless,
I'm left with another gaping hole to fill.
My son should fill it.
He doesn't.

I am a horrible mother.

four

Don't believe me?
   Here's an example of my stellar parenting:

I take acid with some friends
   even though my son is home.
      Sleeping, but home.

I crawl into bed with him and cry as worry and fear devour me.
   What if he needs me?
   What if something happens and
      I have to drive him somewhere?
   What was I thinking?

            What have I done?

I wake the next day, and it's Easter morning. I forgot to hide his eggs. He's too young to know. But I know.

            I'll always know.

He's tugging on my shirt to drag me out of bed.
    I clasp his tiny fingers in mine, so soft and warm and
            innocent.
    He deserves so much better.
    So much better than me.
        I kiss his hand, and he giggles.

Wake up, mommy,
    he says.

I love you,
    I say. I think I mean it.

I'm scraping the dregs of consciousness while he
    plays on the floor.

Terrible, despicable mother.

five

These are the things I look back on years later
as I try to decipher
how I got this way.

What led me here?
Why does it all hurt so much *all the time?*
Nothing f i l l s t h e v o i d .
Nothing curbs the screaming inside.
Nothing silences the whispers.

I find faith, I think. But even that lets me down.
God lets me down.
My church lets me down.
Family and friends let me down.

And *I* let me down.
The whole world is a giant disappointment.
A gaping cavity of torment and suffering.

I think what I wanted more than anything,
    W h a t   I   n e e d e d
        (at least now when I look back)
                    was to feel protected.

From him. From her. From them.

To matter enough to be safeguarded. Stood up for.
    Rescued?

A knight in shining armor, arrived just in time to slay the dragon.

I always did love fairy tales.
    Maybe because I longed so much to be saved from
        Rapunzel's tower,
            Cinderella's wicked stepmother,
                Gaston's blatant innuendo.

The confusion of half the time being told I'm annoying, my ears
stick out too far, my nose is huge, I'm a klutz, too much, too
dramatic…
    and the other half being shoulder-squeezed and
        ogled by old men
            was bound to throw me into turmoil.

Would my path have been a different one if I'd felt that
    sense of security?

I can't really say.
    Nothing can change what has already happened.
        Mistakes were made on all sides,
            and this is where it has left me.

six

Then one day, I stumble upon my Beast.
  My Prince Charming.

Don't get me wrong. We have our chaos parade.
  And it's *bad*. (So, so bad.)

Heroin is his drug of choice. And selfishness.
  He's broken, too.

Sobriety has never looked better on a single, beautiful soul.
  You can argue, but you'll never convince me otherwise.

He is a masterpiece.

As I walk this path through my memories, trying to discern
      why   why   why
  my world has always spun the wrong way,
      its axis tilted at the wrong angle, he listens.

16

Comforts.

        Cares.

                Soothes.

When I fall

        off
        the
        world,

he picks up the slack. Holds my hair. Wipes my tears.
    Never asks when I'll be past it. Never threatens to leave.
    Never makes me feel lesser for it.
    In fact,

        He's proud of me.

What does that even mean?
    How could anyone be proud of the absolute disaster
        I've become?

A miracle. In more ways than one.
    He is my miracle.

I thought I knew what love was

        ugly
             a lie
                manipulation
                    disaster

only made for fairy tales.

I was wrong.

seven

In the years leading up to this terrible period of rebirth,
                      (between the before and the after)
    God calls me back to church.
          I give up (most of) my bad habits,
          I get involved in my church community,
          I read my bible every day. (I try, at least.)
          I cut out entertainment with bad messages. (Easy. Ish.)
          Cut out drinking and drugs. (Mostly.)
          Cut out friends who are bad influences. (A few.)
          Quit my job to homeschool my son. (I'll never regret it.)
          Throw out all of my witchcraft books and supplies.
                (And other temptations.)

Turn my entire life around. (Or at least give the impression of.)

I try to do everything right.
    I work *so hard*.
    Check all the boxes of what it means to be a
             "good Christian."

I am positive this will make me happy.

I have finally found the answer. The *right* path.

But as is often the case with a works-based mindset, I don't quite measure up.

    I don't even realize how much I'm faking it.

        Forcing it.

            Lying to myself.

                    fightingfightingfighting

I am so sure I have it all figured out.

Like Icarus,

    I escape imprisonment with wax-coated wings.

        I rise high

            then crash and burn

                trying to fly too close to the sun.

I expect God to fix me (as He promises to do), and when He doesn't, when it's all still the same, when it still hurts *so much*…

I become inconceivably angry.

    I am angry at the world. (Why do people suck so much?)

    I am angry at my church. (Where is their passion?)

    I am angry God. (Why can't I feel Him?)

    Then.

    I am angry at   m y s e l f .

        (What's wrong with me? Why am I *never* happy?)

And so, as previously stated, I fall off the world.

    Hit pause.

        Quit life.

    Old habits quickly return with abandon.

    A pack of cigarettes and a half-gallon of Tanqueray

    are the cure to stop me feeling everything I don't want to feel.

I know I need to talk to someone. To figure all this out.
    To understand. To heal?
    So I do.
    Twice a week.
                    I t ' s   i n t e n s e .
    And insane.
            Heightens everything I'm already feeling.

I hhhhaaaatttttteeeeee it.

Quick side note:
    I'm so grateful to the man who met with me, counseled,
coached, allowed me to shout, allowed me to cry. Allowed me to
show him the deepest darkest parts of myself and (somehow)
looked back at me without judgement.
    Thank you. I wouldn't be where I am today if not for you.

Back to my story:
    As I drink myself to oblivion,
    the only way I know how to deal with processing
    the pain of being touched that I've never touched,

                    he is there. (My Beast.)

    He loves me anyway,
    tells me I deserve it.

This love.

Tells me I am beautiful,
        amazing,
                lovely,
                            s t r o n g .

What?
    Maybe he's the insane one after all.

I cry harder. Cringe away from his kind words.

The whispers scream how wrong he is, providing
    vibrant examples to
        validate this point.

I listen to them.
    They devour me.
        Blocking out every compliment,
            every happy thought.

Like a sandstorm in the desert, they swallow me whole,
    burn my eyes, cut my skin,
        make my throat raw,
            and bury me beneath piles of debris.

He asks what my mind said in response to his kind words.
    I am too ashamed to tell him.

eight
Masquerade

I gaze in the mirror and say hello
To the altered reflection of the me I know
A fabrication risen from the trenches below
Her insides as filthy as the blackest crow

Once bright eyes darkened by pressure and pain
Bring on the thunder because here comes the rain
Her expression looks wicked, seductive, insane
A villainous smile serves to cover the stain

As I glare back, my stomach churns with disgust
A devil awakened promising destruction and lust
Is the real me still here if I tear back the crust
Or have I wandered astray, lost in lonely distrust

Internally filled with disappointment and rage
Adrift in this cycle like I'm trapped in a cage
Faking a smile, a charade on a stage
Absorbed and untamed in my own masquerade

The mirror holds no fallacies, it sees what I lack
A mirage of one slipping through tedious cracks
Assemble my weapons, I'm under attack
Don't ever surrender to the girl looking back

nine

In those days, that horrid year of agony and rebirth,
    grocery stores send me into a tizzy. All crowds, really.
        People, in general.

But there is one thing that brings me peace.
    Aside from his eyes. His skin against mine.
        Our fingers intertwined.

I go back to my roots and find my way to the woods.
    Pain in my early adulthood (physical pain, I mean)
        kept me from adventuring
            like I used to.

        Sugar is *actual* poison, did you know?

Now, I can't wait to wander beneath the trees.
    My world is shrouded in darkness, but amongst roots and
mushrooms and moss
    I find life,

       healing,
              …peace?

I run my fingers along the tree bark,
    discover new plants and critters,
    learn what a fiddlehead is and when to find them.

I hike mountains until I'm gasping for breath,
    let waterfalls soak me from above,
        skip rocks,
            climb trees,
                smell flowers,
                    admire the sunlit patterns on the forest floor.

I trade shoes for bare feet.
        Work for play.
          Hiding for healing.

Okay, I'm still hiding (Thank you, Gin.), but at least I'm facing
things, right?
    I'm learning. I'm growing. I'm healing.
        I don't even see it happening.
            Can't see it. Not from where I am.

I'm grasping at anything that makes me feel alive.
    I scream at God. Cry to Him.
        Thank Him for His glorious creation
                and my newly-sparked connection to it.

I buy two kayaks that year.
    I grow strong.
        I learn to put them both up on my tiny Neon
                a l l   b y   m y s e l f ,

ratchet straps and yoga mats keeping them in place.

Flask in my bag, I take to the creeks.
    It's just as soothing as a hike,
            more so because of the water on my toes and
                the sunlight on my bare skin.
    I'm like a plant fighting to bloom.

It's life-giving. Life-altering.

And part of me begins to realize that maybe…
    just maybe…

                I might deserve it.

ten

My parents divorce when I am too young to know the difference.
    I spend my life thinking this doesn't affect me since
             it's all I've ever known.

During my year of self-discovery, my awakening,
    my snapinstance—as a beautiful friend of mine calls it,
    I learn so much about myself.
               (Hence calling it my *year of self-discovery.*)

I search the caverns of my heart,
    dig through the trenches and the mud,
        and learn a few things about why my soul aches.

One thing I learn is that

               divorce   sucks

    for the children.
    Wrecks them.
    Damages them like a corrupted cell and
        alters their path forever.

Not all, perhaps, but I'm willing to bet the vast majority are changed in ways that can never be undone.

For me, it's about belonging.
   I never belong anywhere—manifesting my constant
                                    n e e d   t o   f i t   i n .

I am never important, not really. Never needed.

I have two houses, yet both function perfectly without me.
   Two families, yet it feels like I toe the line of both,
              never truly
                    belonging to either.

A family should be whole.
   One unit.
   Father, mother, children.

I have two of everything.
   Two bikes.
   Two Gameboys.
   Two sets of Barbies.

   Two fathers   Two fathers
      Two mothers   Two mothers
         Two siblings   Two siblings

               Two complete homes.

   And only one   M   E.

eleven

The third wheel, if you will.

Just like I am that night on the scratchy carpet as the guy I'm seeing fondles my friend.

Like I am standing next to her.
    She knows everyone. I am rarely introduced.
        I am a side note.
    Not important enough to be called upon.

Like I am when he (a different *he*) tells me he loves me,
    lures me back
        over and over and over,
    (Are you sensing a pattern?)
            then returns to his girlfriend of two years.

I think I love him, too. I think the fact he can't stay away
    despite his relationship
           makes me special.

I thought I knew what love was.

Dirty Little Secret is a radio hit.
    It is also my life.
        I am always a

                    dirty
                         little
                                secret.

Third.

Not once important enough to be first.

twelve

At least when my hero (my miracle, my Beast) puts me second,
   it's to himself
            rather than another woman.
   His own urges.
   His own selfishness.
         And heroin.
            Or whatever addiction he happens to be
               dealing with at the time.

My miracle. Saved by the blood of Jesus.
   Just like me.

And yet…here we are. Still human.
   Still wading through this junked up world.
      It's a muddy river, and I'm in nothing but a towel.
         Bare feet sink into sludge. Dirt splatters my face.

At least we have each other now.

         At least I truly know what love is.

Sometimes, the thought of losing him hurts so much
    I can't take it.
        Tears prick my eyes as I write these words.

It's terrifying.
    He's only human.
            He thinks he's Superman,
                    but despite being my hero, he isn't Superman.

(He did die once, but that doesn't count.)

Sometimes, I worry God will test me by taking him away.
    God is supposed to be my number one.
            My Best Friend. My Comfort. My Savior. My Rock.

He's not.
    I still don't trust Him like I should.

He let all of this horrible stuff happen, didn't He?
    Where was He?

I love Him. I think.   (I think I know what love is?)

But I love my best friend more.
    My husband.
        My soulmate.

I know it's a sin.
    And dangerous.
        It could all fall apart in the blink of an eye.

God does like to test us, doesn't He?

thirteen

These words make me sound cynical.
    Maybe even like I'm not the Christian

I   c l a i m   t o   b e.

Sorry to break it to you, but all Christians are hypocrites.
    We all preach to be something no one can ever live up to.
            But still, we strive.

Sinful. Broken. Disgusting.

Being a Christian doesn't make you perfect.
    And it shouldn't make you judge and jury either.
        Being a Christian means loving God and loving people.

            (I suck at both…but I'm trying.)

I feel closer to God now than I ever have before.
    I spend time with Him.

I worship Him. Church twice a week. Study His Word.
        Even teach it sometimes.
It's different than before, when I was faking it.
When I was forcing it.
        I think it's different.

I long for heaven more than anything I've ever longed for

                in   my   life.

Paradise.
    Rivers flowing with milk and honey.
    A new body.
    Restored.
    A new earth.
    Remade.
    No longer east of Eden but   *immersed*   *in*   *it.*

                    Home.

But here on earth…this foul, polluted, poisonous rock….

                it often feels like my best friend is my lifeline.

fourteen

I would like to note this here, for the record:

Lord, please don't take my husband away from me.

fifteen

Let's talk about prayer.
       How do you pray?

I think I have a weird opinion about prayer, and I truly don't
know if it's right or wrong, but it's what I believe.

First, I don't believe in praying for healing.
    Did your mouth just drop open?
        I said what I said.

Some consider this "weak Christianity." And maybe it is.
    Maybe years from now, I'll write another book about
        my newfound belief in the power of prayer.

But as of now, a decade back walking with God,
    I struggle with trusting its efficacy.
    If God already knows everything,
        then how will my prayers really make a difference?

Still, I pray to be obedient, and I pray to connect with God.
  I pray God's will over a situation.
            (Please excuse my hypocrisy in the previous chapter.)

I pray He will bring comfort, wisdom, peace,
  pain-relief, and that He will use every situation for good.

Sometimes, I even pray for people to die, knowing they are going
to heaven and will be happier there.
  (Sick people, I mean. Not just…perfectly healthy people.)

If I don't think they are going to heaven or I'm not sure,
        I pray their tragedy leads to salvation,

                  their's or someone else's.

I don't pray for God to take away your aunt's flu;
  I pray for her comfort until it passes.

I don't pray for a child to make it through surgery;
  I pray for wisdom for the doctors, steady hands,
          peace for the parents,
                  and a speedy recovery,
                        should it be God's will they survive.

(More hypocrisy coming at you: Despite feeling this way, I am
not above bargaining with God when I'm feeling desperate.
When my son was put under anesthesia for surgery, I reminded
God of all the ways my life would be blown to smithereens if I
lost him. So this "pray for God's will" thing isn't a perfect system,
but it is what I strive for.)

I don't ask God for what   I   think my future should be;
      (Though I sometimes give him ideas.)
  I ask Him to show me the path He has laid out for me
  so I don't stumble through the wilderness on my own.
      To make the way clear and to
          hold my hand as I hack through the thorns.

To give me strength when I'm resistant to His plans.
  To give me courage to face His enemies.

I don't ask God for the things *I* think should happen.
  I ask for the comfort only He can give as
      His Will plays out.

Most often I ask that He help me feel
          peace that surpasses all understanding.

Sometimes I ask to feel nothing at all.

I haven't always thought this way. I used to beg God for things to
work out the way   I   thought they should.
  (Don't judge me. I'm only human.)

The closer I get to God, the more I realize that while I'm sitting
in the driver's seat, Jesus is my copilot.

        The blessed, coveted shotgun seat.

  It's the shotgun's job to navigate
             and to pick the music.

sixteen

The truth is, no matter how much I learn about myself and
    why I am the way that I am,
                it doesn't change *who* I am. It doesn't fix it.

    Doesn't fix *me*.

Like wearing floaties in an ocean.
    You know, those horrible, rubber ones that stick to your skin.
        A blood-pressure cuff for toddlers.

Sure, I'm floating with these giant, orange, inflatable
    bands around my arms.

Kind of floating.
        My arms are floating, at least.

                Sometimes my head still slides under.

I try every single day to be better,
    kinder, less cynical.
        To love, to trust, to be patient.

    Lovejoypeacepatiencekindnessgoodnessfaithfulnessgentleness
        andselfcontrol.

I try,
    I beg,
        for these fruits to be alive in me,
          for the Spirit to be alive in me,
            for passion to be alive in me.

Does God answer? I'm honestly not sure.
    I long for what lies on the other side of heaven
        where the grass truly is greener,
            (Also milk and honey!)
        and I know I'll never have that here.

The more I write, the more this feels like a suicide note.
    I can tell you with absolute certainty—it is not.

I have joy here on planet earth. My husband is my joy. My son.

My books (both the ones I read and the ones I write—
            though perhaps not this one)
        and the fantastical worlds I find within them.

Art brings me joy.
    My fake fireplace surrounded by bookshelves.
    Cooking dinner for my best friend.

Playing games.
Watching my boys spend time together.
Sunshine. The forest. The trees.
Discovering mushrooms hidden along the trail.
Flowers blooming.
The plants above my sink sprouting new leaves.
My kitties.
The miniature library I'm constructing from a box.
Anime.

I read fantasy, watch plants grow, and enjoy anime.

That should be a t-shirt.

seventeen

More than anything else, I desire
                    c o n n e c t i o n .

I desire friendship, companionship, love.
        And I *loathe* small talk. All those impersonal,
                                passionless,
                                dare I say *fake?*
                                        conversations.

When I connect with you, I want to talk about
                    your beliefs,
                    the things you love,
                    what brings you joy,
                    your traumas and mistakes,
                    questions you have about the universe,
                    stories that spoke to you,
                    your struggles and addictions,
                    the music that moves you,
                    conspiracy theories,
                    experiences that touched your heart.

Despite these desires,
 I haven't had the best of luck with friends.
                         (As you may have noticed.)

They hurt me.
 I hurt them.
 Don't think I claim innocence.

At one point, I was so set on self-destructing,
        so craving to feel special
                 so determined to prove I was worth something

I slept with one of my closest friend's ex-boyfriends.
                 (Recent ex.)

And worse than that, they still loved each other.
 I knew it.
 He knew it.
 I was whacked out of my mind on pills.
         He didn't know that.
 She was heartbroken.
                         Who wouldn't be?

We have barely spoken a word to each other since then. If you're
reading this, though I doubt you are, I'm sorry. I know I owe so
many people so many apologies.

So don't think this is intended as some pity party.
 I made my fair share of mistakes
                 when it came to friendships.
 Usually where boys were concerned, but not always.

Like Papa Roach shouted from the rooftops,

I just want To Be Loved!

Is that too much to ask?
    Maybe not. But my system for feeling loved is
            disastrously flawed.
    (Can't imagine why.)

As I've grown,
    gotten married,
        found home in my family
            and a place in God's Kingdom (I think?),
    I've gotten better at not *destroying* relationships.

Still, they elude me.
    Even now, my best friend (other than my husband)
        lives on another continent for most of the year.

People I've grown close to have
    abandoned me
        for seemingly no reason,
            though I imagine there must be one.

Likely the result of my stunning personality.

I know *abandoned* is a dramatic word,
    but that's how it feels.
    When you meet with someone for months on end
        and then suddenly…nothing.
            What else would you call it?

My siblings and I are so different. We have so little in common
and are at totally different stages and walks in life.

I'm close with my mother, which is a blessing.

And there are a few other people I feel a deeper connection to.
    The problem is, I am so damaged that I'm terrified
            to let most people get too close.

(It's part of why I'm so afraid to publish this book.
                    Those who love me are likely to read it.)

When they (or anyone) see the depths of me,
                the truth of me,
        they'll run away,
            like so many others have before them.

I have tried to find companionship online.
    Like-minded people!
    When I jump on Facebook and see people *actually* responding
        to the things I say,
            actually sparking conversation,
                the dopamine boost is fantastic.
                            I AM LOVED!

But then when I get on to stretches of zero notifications…
    (We're all fighting the algorithm, right?)
                    …it's discouraging. Even saddening.

Not to mention the small talk that often ensues.
    Faux congratulations and meaningless conversations with the
        ultimate intention of boosting views.

It's appreciated, but it's not the totality of what I'm looking for.

This is the problem with social media.
    It mimics connection,
        mirrors it.

But it is a falsehood. A deception.
    Like so many other things.
        Like me.

eighteen

Mirror

Will I ever become who I desire to be?
A woman pristine, lovely, and clean.
Gaze in the mirror. Do you enjoy what you see?
Peering back, is she who you wish to be?

Is she out there? Lost? Will she ever be found?
This imposter residing unworthy a crown.
Chains jangle around me, I'm eternally bound.
To struggle and drown as these snares drag me down.

I seek one that flourishes with kindness and love.
With strength that can only be found from above.
A heart filled with hope and peace like a dove.
Does she even exist? This girl I'm dreaming of?

Regret who I was, despise what I am.
The broken shell I possess, never part of the plan.
Like a bird out searching, praying for land.
How long will I wait with outstretched hands?

A ship with no compass, no map, lost at sea.
Stumbling, tumbling, attempting to flee.
Lord, will you help me? I beg to be free.
Will I ever find that "she" I am longing to be?

nineteen

Despite feeling differently about it now
    I did try to kill myself before.
    Twice, actually.

I was younger then.
    Don't judge me.

Now I'm working on leveling my hormones and freeing myself
from the pockets of Big Pharma.

                And getting closer to God, of course.

The True Healer.

        The Great Physician.

The first time— Zoloft.

STOP

GIVING

IT

TO

CHILDREN.

So many studies point to a rise in suicidal ideation when taking it,
so WHY is it even an option?

Balance your adolescents' hormones instead of giving them
faulty serotonin and dopamine.
Balance your own hormones!

Learn/teach coping skills and healthy habits.
Stop eating junk.
Practice less screen time.
Stabilize your sleeping patterns.
Get some therapy.

That is not to say anti-depressants are never needed or useful,
but (in my opinion) it's not nearly as often as the pharmaceutical
companies would have you believe.
(And they pay big money to ensure doctors are taught
exactly what they want them to teach, right?)

Anyway. Zoloft.
    I take 25.
    But not all at once.
        I'm scared, okay?

This is also the first time I touch a man's…you know.
    Parts.

It is not enjoyable.

I had one boyfriend before this, but we only touched over jeans,
    which doesn't really count.

That night,
    he's wearing pajama pants.
    He's my brother's friend, did I mention?
    We are all in the basement watching a movie.
    He and I are on the couch, my legs stretched between us.
    I'm thirteen.
    I think?

He uses my foot to…you know.
    It feels disgusting. I don't know what to do.
        I'm ashamed, horrified.

        I'm also high as a kite.
            And polite.

My brother sees and flips his lid.
    We never speak of it again.

The next day I'm taken to the hospital, stomach pumped.
    Everyone wants to know why.

                    Why
                            Why
                                    Why

Have you looked around? Do you see this place?
    Two dads
    Two moms
    Two siblings (times 2)

Broken. Never had a chance at being whole.

I'm sad, I guess. Is that what this feeling is?
        This dismal despair? This hopelessness?

I went to church.
    I heard about heaven.
        I thought I held the key to the door.

(25 keys)

Black charcoal on my lips, they suck me dry.
    Keys, stolen.
    I'm stuck here.

I'm sent to a hospital for others like me.

                    Everyone there is   I N S A N E .

I clearly don't belong.
　　I'm just sad.

I never belong.
　　Not even in a mental hospital…apparently.
　　Maybe it's me. Maybe I'm the problem.
　　Maybe I don't fit because
　　　　　　　　　　　　　　　I don't want to.

Now THAT'S insane.

The walls are white. There's no color anywhere.
　　Everything is white and neat and clean, and it amplifies
　　　　　　t h e　　　c h a o s
　　I feel inside.

My roommate talks to herself. Or to no one.
　　Or to demons, maybe.
　　　　So, at least I don't do that.

I go back later, to this same hospital
　　but this time I'm in the adult wing.
　　　　　　　Though I was only 18.
　　　　　　　　　　　Does that actually make an adult?

I stopped taking my pills. Lexapro, if memory serves.
　　Three days is all it took for me to crack.
　　I lose it on my family.

RAGERAGERAGE.

My father slaps me across the face.
    He's never done that before.
    Or since.

I'm used to abuse at this point,
                    (From that boyfriend. You know the one.)
        so it doesn't really phase me.

It isn't my dad's fault I'm off my rocker.

Is it?

This time, I take all my pills.
    Even those sweet little sugar babies.
    I carve my boyfriend's initials into my arm (to say goodbye).

The sperm donor, in case you aren't keeping up.
    How could you?

I leave him a note to hide all of my Wiccan books so as not to
    disappoint my family after my death.

I'm searching for peace.
    Always searching, never quite reaching.

I drive 2.2 miles. Totally blacked out.
    No memory at all.
        They find me parked in a no-parking zone.

I tried really hard to get to heaven that day.

I failed.

Thank God.

twenty

My point is this:
    (Surely I'll get to it eventually, right?)
    As much as I long for *home*, I won't be heading there of my own accord.

Still, this world is a dark, confusing, and nasty place.
    Everything is so broken and messed up.

I am a conspiracy theorist through and through.
    (I blame Santa. But that's a story for another time.)

Since Covid, I'm not even sure you can call us *theorists* anymore.
    Conspiracy Truth-Tellers.
        Sages of the Twenty-First Century.

Even if the world doesn't want to see.

I won't deep-dive into my realm of pessimistic *theories* about the world at large,

but I have them.
        I see the deception and blindness and corruption.

And yet within this darkness and brokenness, we are to be the
   l i g h t   o f   t h e   w o r l d ,
   the city on a hill,
   the candle that lets its light shine.

Physically
   We will be persecuted.
   We will be scorned.
   We will be killed—like a lamb to the slaughter.

Spiritually
   We will be oppressed.
   We will be tormented.
   We will be the enemy's target.

So God, I ask You this:

How are we supposed to be both?
   a light amongst the darkness
   whole amongst the broken
   loving amongst the cruel

It's a contradiction.

   we are dark
   we are broken
   we are cruel

Your grace is enough, You claim.

But what does that mean?

What is *enough?*

> *Send out your light and your truth; let them guide me. Let*
> *them lead me to your holy mountain, to the place where you*
> *live. There I will go to the altar of God, to God—the source*
> *of all my joy. I will praise you with my harp, O God,*
> *my God!*
>
> *Psalm 43:3-4*

twenty-one

We work so hard, but what do we gain?

Money, a clean house, an education, a pretty garden, friends, a successful business, a muscular body, an impressive portfolio.

But what does it all mean? What does it *matter?*

We live, and then we die, but the world keeps spinning.
    We are like the wind,
            going
                    going
                            going
                                    like a hamster in a wheel.

We keep trying to fill ourselves up
    but we are never full.
            Never satisfied.

Because only Christ can truly satisfy our soul.

And it's our soul that's aching
                        longing
                                yearning
                                        craving.

We are born desiring Jesus. Every single one of us.
    Whether you believe in Him or not,
            the thirst is innate.

And powerful. So powerful we try every possible way we
    can think of to satiate that hunger.
        Sex
                drugs
                        rock and roll.
                                Among other things.

        But   o n l y   Jesus can fill it.

Sin entered the world in the garden and spread
                                infected
                                contaminated
                                polluted
                                poisoned
                                imprisoned
                                infested
                                caged

permeated the very depths of us

                        and separated us from God.

Here comes the good news:

> God loved us so much
> > He sent Jesus to set us all free.

Jesus is the key to heaven.
> > > The only key.

He paid the price on our heads with his human life, and in turn,
we are granted access to eternal life with our true Father.
> Our Creator.

Does knowing this make life easy?
> > No.

Does believing it to be true in the very core of my being make
me feel it 100% of the time?
> > No.

Life is hard.
> We are sinful creatures living in a sinful world.
> But even in the depths of my
> > sorrow
> > > anger
> > > > fear
> > > > > worry
> > > > > > mistrust

Knowing Jesus has given me   h o p e
> > for the first time in my life.

twenty-two

Do you ever feel God's pull on your heart?
    I can always tell when it's Him because
        the thing I feel compelled to do
            makes me *super* uncomfortable.

                            Or defiant. Or angry.

(A little like how I feel about writing and releasing this book!)

To be honest, I get angry a lot.

I fight it. (This thing. Not my anger. Though I fight that, too.)
    Tooth and nail.
        Sans violence, of course.

One way God has coached me is in my worship.
    Put up your hands, He says.

I don't want to. It's embarrassing.
    Especially if most people around me aren't doing it.

Do it anyway, He says. *Help them see.*

No.
    Nonononono.

Then He says, *It isn't about them, it's about Me.*

At last, I give in.
    It's freeing.

Well, at first it's terrifying,
    then it's freeing.
    Life is funny like that, isn't it?
    That first jump is always frightening, then comes the freefall.

Next He says, *Worship Me on your knees.*

No.   Way.
    Why? No one else is doing it! What will people think?
    Will they think I'm weird? A fraud? Dramatic?
    I can worship You just fine on my feet. Look at my hands.

                They're up so high.

It will mean more, He says. *To Me. To you.*

I will absolutely onehundredpercent NOT drop to my knees in a room full of people.
    No.

You will. Then you'll see.

The first time I give in, I emerge from my time of worship
    in a daze.
    So filled with love for my God.
    With reverence.

If you've never been on your knees before God,
    I highly recommend it.

My God is so great!

He holds us together,
    literally every molecule in the universe is held in His hands.

    human
    animal
    mineral
    the ocean
        THE OCEAN
    plants
    earthairfirewater
    and every single star.

Because He wills it, they exist.
    Isn't that incredible?
        It's unfathomable.

Our puny, human brains can't begin to comprehend
    the depth of that.

He deserves our worship.
    My worship. My obedience.
    So, I try to do what He wants me to do.
    Even when it's scary, weird, not what everyone else is doing.
        Even when it's hard.
            Even when it makes me angry.

I am His vessel. I am *His*.

But regardless of how hard I try to will my motives into
    submission,
        sometimes my worship is selfish. My obedience in selfish.

I obey to get things from Him. To win His favor.

        I worship to feel better.

    Peace.
    Belonging.
    Important.
    Loved.

I thought I knew what love was.
    I guess I'm still figuring it out.

        Maybe I'll never truly understand it east of Eden.

twenty-three

You know the old adage that says if you're ever lost in the woods,
    stay put until someone finds you?

Sometimes, I find myself there in life,
    not on a grand scale
    (usually)
    but in a moment so consuming,
        I can do nothing more than sit
              exactly   where   I   am

           and wait for someone to come find me.

When I first find myself stationary,
    I have every intention of taking a breath and reanimating,
    good as new.

But then the whispers descend,
        and I spiral.

The decision to stop and wait isn't really a conscious one,
      though I can't deny that I do imagine someone will come
            eventually
      and break me from Medusa's snare.

Sometimes they do.
      Sometimes they don't.
            Sometimes it's up to me to
                  rise
                  from
                  the
                  ashes

                        and move forward.

How long do I sit and wait and hope?
      How many whispers from the devil consume me
      during that time?
      Making me sadder and angrier.

It depends on the day.
      The incident that brought me there.

And sometimes, even when I rise,

                        I still feel lost.

twenty-four

Where would I be without You?

Sometimes I look back with anger at all You allowed me to go through.

But with eyes wide open, I can look back at all the

t w i s t s   and   t u r n s

of life and see Your hand in it.

All the times I could have died,
    should have died, would have died.
        Not just the on-purpose times.

You are there.
    You step in.
    Even when I don't see You,

even when I reject You,
even when I don't feel it AT ALL,
even when the oceans rise around me,
even when I ignore you,
even when my life is in absolute turmoil,

like the Hebrews in the desert, you free me…rescue me.
Over and over and over again.

You are so worthy of praise. So kind.
So good.
The King of the Mountain
The Shepherd in the Valley
The Creator of the Universe
The Maker of Every Good Thing

Jehovah Shalom
The Lord is Peace

Adonai
Sovereign Ruler, Master

Elohim
God the Creator

El Roi
The God Who Sees Me

El Shaddai
Almighty God

Yahweh Rohi
> The Lord is my Shepherd

Jehovah Rapha
> The Lord Who Heals

Yahweh Tsuri
> The Lord is My Rock

Immanuel
> God With Us

Jehovah Jireh
> The Lord Will Provide

You will provide.
> Your grace is enough.

> YOU   ARE   ENOUGH.

So why do I still find it hard to trust You?
> Why do I still feel lost? Forgotten? Astray?

twenty-five

You hurt me.
You let them hurt me.
You let me hurt me.

Why?

Why, at times, is it so freaking hard to feel You?
To hear Your voice?
To know You're there.

I want to trust You with my whole heart,
but I don't even trust *him* with my whole heart,
(my best friend)
so how could I trust You?

I can't feel You.
I can't see You.
I can't touch You.

You never hold my hand,
    never hold me in Your arms,
    never whisper truths I both loathe and long to hear.

Sometimes, You feel so far away.
    And I feel lost.

Sometimes, it's like You're the breath in my lungs,
    the oxygen keeping me going.
    (Yes, I know *technically* You are,
                    but I'm talking about feelings, not science.)

We aren't supposed to chase feelings. I know this.
    But YOU gave us these feelings, didn't You?
        We are made in YOUR image.
            Pulled from the dust of the earth
                with Your breath in our lungs.

Why did you give us the capacity for feelings we
    aren't supposed to live by?
    Why did you make them so potent if we
        aren't to be led by them?

Is it sin that ruined them?
            Did Adam and Eve have more manageable feelings
                before the fall?

Sometimes I have so many feelings inside me
    I think I might   s p o n t a n e o u s l y   c o m b u s t .
        (That's a real fear, by the way. I watched an
            Unsolved Mystery as a kid, and it traumatized me.)

But feelings…they swallow me up.
　　Smash me against the rocks like an ocean tide against a cliff.
　　Consume me like the serpent living in the deep,
　　　　dark waters below.

And I don't know how to combat them.
　　I try to speak Your truth,
　　read Your Word,
　　worship.

Sometimes it helps,
　　　　　　but often, the whispers remain.

twenty-six

The devil
    is excellent
        at prodding old wounds.

He knows us so well, knows *me* so well.
    Knows exactly how to play the board so he can
        pierce my heart the exact right way to break me.

I try not to let him. I really do.
    Sometimes I win.
                Sometimes...I don't.

Do you ever notice that the same things come up
    over and over again?
        The same fears
            struggles
                addictions
                    longings

                        sins.

This is not a coincidence. He knows how to hurt you.
  He wants to Destroy you,
            to Devour you,
            to Demolish your family,
            to Dismantle your ministry,
            to Devastate your heart beyond repair.

He is a big D.
  A devil, I mean.
  These are his goals.
            Sound familiar?

Do you ever feel left out? Forgotten? Ignored?
  This is one of my big ones. (Remember?…belonging.)

It happens to me   a l l   t h e   t i m e.

So often that I have now come to realize the only logical
explanation is that the devil blinds my friends and family to this.
They don't even realize they do it.
  I'm not being left out or forgotten
  because they don't care
  but because *he* knows it cuts me.

Maybe you think I'm rationalizing.
  Maybe I am.

But I also know this: people
  (especially people who care about me)
            don't usually *set out* to hurt me.

That doesn't mean it doesn't hurt.

Even though I believe this to be the case, sometimes I still drown in self-pity and question everything I've come to learn about love, friendship, family, and my own self-worth.

It's a wound he stabs constantly. Because he knows it works.

What wounds does he prod in you?
What scars does he rip open every chance he gets?
What temptations does he then dangle in front of you the moment you've broken down?

Knowledge is power. Awareness is power.
Pay attention.
Look for the signs.

Know your enemy. He certainly knows you.

twenty-seven

Fervent

Satan can't be everywhere, that much I know is true.

But his army of angry demons and darkness live to smother you.

First he'll bite your passion,
    that spiritual flame you hold inside.
    He'll snuff out your desire so in God you won't confide.

Disheveling your focus so you won't see his ugly face.
    You'll think your fighting for a cause
    when you should be giving grace.

Your identity he'll come for next, overwhelming you with doubt,
    so you feel so lost and insecure you can't find your way out.

Hold tight to your family, there's a target on their heads,
    dividing them in chaos while they sleep soundly
    in their beds.

Past mistakes will haunt you as your confidence he breaks.
   He'll play that broken record swearing
   judgement at the gates.

He'll amplify your fears, for fear consumes us all.
   Our deafening anxieties are drowning out God's call.

Tempting you with darkness, masquerading it with light.
   Corrupting all your inner truths until you've given up the
fight.

He'll overload your world with tasks, distract at every turn,
   suffocate with life's demands so to God you won't return.

Your heart he beats the hardest, at least that's true with mine.
   Anger, pain, and bitterness devouring my mind.

He tears apart relationships so you feel all alone,
   disrupting your community and ripping up your home.

Jesus is our Savior. He delivers from the beast.
   Hold tight to Him so one day you will join His holy feast.

Be fervent in your prayers. He's the one to help you through.
   Pick up your shield and know God's word,
   I'm on my guard, are you?

twenty-eight

Don't just know your enemy, know God, too.
　　Love like Jesus.
　　Let the Holy Spirit live your life for you.
　　This is something I see lacking in the "American church."
　　Some churches are like the Corinthians, putting too much
focus on the Holy Spirit and lifting themselves up in the process
with all of their tongues and healing and prophecy.

Don't get me wrong—I believe in miracles.
　　I sleep next to one every night.
　　But some take it too far.

Then we have the opposite end of the spectrum, where
everything is tradition and going through the motions.

　　　　　Church once a week, the end.
　　　　　　　No genuine worship.
　　　　　　　No time in the Word.
　　　　　　　No prayer.
　　　　　　　No witness.

God is a sidenote,
    a to-do to be checked off a list.
    One hour a week.
    Okay, maybe two, but God forbid we run over our
            scheduled time slot.
                    Nope. Time's UP. Everybody go home.

If you practice these behaviors, is the Spirit really leading you?

Is the Spirit leading me?
    I like to think He is, but is He really?
    Am I filled with His fruit?
    Am I conscious of my sin?

Sometimes I am so angry I could tear out my hair.
    Sometimes I am so bitter I could drown in it.

I am unhappy. I am discontent.

Does that really sound like someone led by the Spirit?
    No. It doesn't.
    So while I sit here on my high horse
    telling you all the ways you should be doing it differently
    know I am the biggest hypocrite of them all.

    I am dark
    I am broken
    I am cruel

Lord, I truly do not understand why You think You can use me.

Or why You would even want to.

I have let You down
           so
                   many
                           times.

Can't You see that?
    Don't You remember?

I let You down today,
                yesterday,
                last week.

                    Every moment I exist, I am failing You.

Show me the right path, O Lord; point out the road for me to follow. Lead me by your truth and teach me, for you are the God who saves me. All day long I put my hope in you. Remember, O Lord, your compassion and unfailing love, which you have shown from long ages past. Do not remember the rebellious sins of my youth. Remember me in the light of your unfailing love, for you are merciful, O Lord.
Psalm 25:4-7

twenty-nine

Yet You keep putting me in these situations that feel
    so intentional.

My book series, for instance.
    How it came out of no where in such a monstrous season.
    A season where I was a monster,
    You were a monster,
    the monsters were inside of me.
    In my head, my thoughts, my actions,
    my dreams, my desires, my longings.

My snapinstance.

And somehow, magically
              (Another miracle?)
    You gave me this incredible story to share with the world,
        to heal me,

             and hopefully heal others, too.

You put people in my path You want to touch, to reach,
and You use ME to reach them.
How? Why?

We are the Island of Misfit Toys, with all our little misfits.
They flock to us,
and I pray they see You in us,
that something about this messed up little existence would
reach their hearts and draw them closer to You.

I am in constant awe of the work I see You doing all around me.
I am constantly validated in the attacks of the enemy.
Why is he trying so hard to destroy us?
Why has he tried so hard my entire life?

I can only think of one reason.

You have big things planned. For me, my family, the people in my
life.
Your people.
Your church.
Your bride.

You have big plans, far beyond our wildest comprehension.
I see it.
I know I say I don't trust You.
(Sometimes I don't.)

But deep down
I see it.

thirty

It's so easy to let the whispers creep in.
                    That's what I call them. Whispers.
         Dark little whispers that infiltrate my mind,
                   corrupt my thoughts,
         pouring out from the deepest trenches of my heart.

E v e r y   s i n g l e   i n s e c u r i t y   I've ever felt.

Song of Solomon calls them *little foxes.*
    I like *whispers* better.

A fox is tangible. I get the metaphor, but it doesn't quite speak to
how it truly feels to have a demon on my shoulder whispering
every insecurity that has been validated my whole life.

No one likes me.
         No one invites me.
               I don't belong anywhere.
                    I don't fit. Not really.
                         I am an outsider.

Not welcome in the inner circle.
I am weird, annoying, *too much*.
Not enough.

Too many emotions, too many issues, too much drama.

He whispers, *See? Yet another confirmation that what you've always
believed about yourself is true. They see what you really are. Stop fooling
yourself. You clearly don't belong here. You aren't wanted. Aren't needed. And
you* d e f i n i t e l y *aren't loved.*

Left behind. Abandoned.
Don't fit in.

I know these things. I feel them so profoundly sometimes.
And they hurt. Like a butter knife to my chest.
Like a weight pinning me to the bottom of
the Mariana Trench.

Will these thoughts and feelings ever go away?
I keep thinking they hold less power over me.
Like I've overcome them.
Then suddenly,
they consume me in whirlwind of despair
I didn't see coming.

It's infuriating, agonizing,
and always there beneath the surface waiting to pounce.

thirty-one

So am I living by the Spirit?
  If I am, why do these thoughts devour me?
  Why do I let these hateful whispers get under my skin?
      Why do they exist at all?

I know I am loved.
  God says I am loved, wanted, His.
      My husband says I am loved, wanted, his.

So why does this keep happening? Why does it hurt
        s o   d a m n   m u c h ?

If the Holy Spirit lives in me,
  I have God with me at all times.
      His light dispels the darkness!
      His power is greater than any in existence!
      His love is unending, never changing, never leaving!
  With Him, in Him, I AM ENOUGH.

Logically, I know this to be true. I even, dare I say, believe it.

But in my heart of hearts, I am broken.
    Despairing
             wandering
                    ashamed
                            fearful
                                    furious
                                            miserable
                                                    discontent.

Things I've done,
    things that have been done to me,

        they are still here…
                hiding in the darkness
                                clawing to break free.

And in my heart of hearts, I am also whole.
    Alive
            breathing
                    free
                  awake
                          comforted
                                  loved.
    More than I have ever been in my entire life.

He is the strength that helps me through each day.
    He pulled me from the absolute despair of my youth,
        and even if it isn't perfect now,
            even if I don't always feel Him,
                    I KNOW He is there.

I have the power to rise against my demons,
    to face them head on.
    In Jesus' name, I stand on solid ground.

thirty-two
I Am Me

I am an artist, painting the desires of my soul.
    The universe is the landscape of my canvas,
        begging to experience my design.

I am the music
    that is the soundtrack to my life.

The rhythm
    that has forced my feet into motion.

The lyrics
    that have eaten away at my being,
        carving trenches through the depths of my emotion.

I am the books I've explored.
    The characters who have engaged me and changed me.

I am every story I've ever heard.

I am the people who have loved me.
                    I am intimacy.   I am passion.
                              I am cherished.

I am the friendships that have blessed me.
        An echo of those special people who have touched my heart
                and the ones who have broken it.

I am the trials that have strengthened me.
        The lessons I've learned   t h e   h a r d   w a y .

I am a journey of progression and regression.

I am the melody of the birds.
        The wind in the trees at the top of a mountain.
                The flames that dance and sway.

I am molded by the places I've been, the things I've seen,
        and all the future adventures I have yet to experience.

I am a reckless dreamer.
                I am a fervent prayer.
                        I am the evolution of my spirit.
                                The ebb and flow of the waves.

                    I am wild.

The glittering of starlight.
        I am the tears that have flooded my cheeks.
                The grief. The trauma produced by this fallen world.

I am the joy of God's creation all around me.

I am beautiful.
I am happiness, love, laughter, and silliness.
I am darkness. I am light.
I am broken. I am healed.
I am fear. I am hope.

I am all of these things woven together.

I am me.

thirty-three

Lord,
>   Glorious Father in Heaven,
>   Jesus My Savior,
>   Spirit so Holy,

I am begging you to save me.
>   Save me from myself. From the depravity of this world.
>   Help me put my whole focus on YOU and nothing else.
>   Help me long to spend every moment with You.
>   Give me a passion for Your Word,
>   confidence in Your Will,
>   clarity in Your World.

Because it is YOUR World. The devil may run amok, but I know the battle is already won. The path is marked, the date set, the plan is already underway.
>   You are victorious!
>   You are the King of kings.
>   Lord of lords.
>   Holy of holies.
>   You are magnificent.
>   You are excited to bring Your children home!

In Your Word, You promise to be my Rock,
                                my Shelter
                                my Comfort
                                my Redeemer
                                my Lover
                                my Father
                                my Friend
                                my Savior
                                my Shepherd
                                my Light
                                my Wisdom
                                my Grace
                                my Shield
                                my Joy
                                my Hope
                                my Refuge
                                my Strength
                                my Truth
                                my Healer
                                my Deliverer
                                my Power
                                my Salvation

                                    my everything,

and so I am asking You to fulfill those promises.
      Help me feel them. Help me believe them.
            Help me know in the depths of my heart that
                  t h e y   a r e   T R U T H .

      I want to seek You and BELIEVE.
      I want to feel You and TRUST.
      I want to ask You and KNOW.

Help my unbelief.

I need You, Lord.
I. Need. You.
Please. Hear me. Help me.
Love me like You promise You will.

And help me feel it.

Amen.

The Lord hears his people when they call to him for help. He rescues them from all their troubles. The Lord is close to the brokenhearted; he rescues those whose spirits are crushed.
Psalm 34:17-18

I will exalt you, my God and King, and praise your name forever and ever. I will praise you every day; yes, I will praise you forever. Great is the Lord! He is most worthy of praise! No one can measure his greatness. Let each generation tell its children of your mighty acts; let them proclaim your power. I will meditate on your majestic, glorious splendor and your wonderful miracles. Your awe-inspiring deeds will be on every tongue; I will proclaim your greatness. Everyone will share the story of your wonderful goodness; they will sing with joy about your righteousness. The Lord is merciful and compassionate, slow to get angry and filled with unfailing love. The Lord is good to everyone. He showers compassion on all his creation. All of your works will thank you, Lord, and your faithful followers will praise you. They will speak of the glory of your kingdom; they will give examples of your power. They will tell about your mighty deeds and about the majesty and glory of your reign. For your kingdom is an everlasting kingdom. You rule throughout all generations. The Lord always keeps his promises; he is gracious in all he does. The Lord helps the fallen and lifts those bent beneath their loads. The eyes of all look to you in hope; you give them their food as they need it. When you open your hand, you satisfy the hunger and thirst of every living thing. The Lord is righteous in everything he does; he is filled with kindness. The Lord is close to all who call on him, yes, to all who call on him in truth. He grants the desires of those who fear him; he hears their cries for help and rescues them. The Lord protects all those who love him, but he destroys the wicked. I will praise the Lord, and may everyone on earth bless his holy name forever and ever.

Psalm 145

afterword

If you made it this far, you may be wondering what in the world to do with everything you just read. I left you on quite a cliffhanger, didn't I? A cry for help. It's a prayer I pray often.

If you know Jesus already, I hope you feel seen. Know you're not alone when you struggle with your walk. We all struggle.

If you don't know Jesus and think you might want to, I hope this encourages you to seek Him. Being a Christian is not easy, but it *is* worth it. It is the only thing that brought me from the beginning of this story to the end. It saved me from that dark world and carried me into the light. The light isn't perfect, but I can say with absolute certainty—it is better.

More than anything else, I want this story to serve as an invitation. I want it to spark revival. In me. In the world. In you. So, if you want to know more about Jesus, reach out. To me, to a friend, to family…to someone. If you want to talk about depression, addiction, suicide, abuse, or anything else, I'll listen. *Someone* will listen.

My inbox is always open. jpietro7716@gmail.com

Thank you for reading.

playlist

1. Head Above Water - Avril Lavigne
2. Hanging On By A Thread - The Letter Black
3. Hard Days - Brantley Gilbert
4. Monster - Skillet
5. Reason Living - Studio Yuraki
6. Us - James Bay
7. I Need Help - Connor Price, Maverick City Music, & Taylor Hill feat. Nick Day
8. dont let me go - Machine Gun Kelly [E]
9. Coming Clean - Hilary Duff
10. You'll Be Alright, Kid - Alex Warren
11. Here Again - Elevation Worship
12. Only Human - Lecrae & BJ The Chicago Kid
13. Hymn of Heaven - Phil Wickham
14. Beautiful Things - Benson Boone
15. Gratitude - Brandon Lake
16. All Around Me - Flyleaf
17. The Search - NF
18. Unfinished - Mandisa
19. There Was Jesus - Zach Williams and Dolly Parton
20. Another in the Fire - Hillsong UNITED
21. Even If - MercyMe
22. Abandoned - Benjamin William Hastings & Brandon Lake

23. On My Own - Ashes Remain
24. Jireh - Cross Point Music
25. Would Anyone Care - Citizen Soldier
26. Hi Ren - Ren [E]
27. Still Waters - Leanna Crawford
28. Still God - Genevieve Linkowski
29. It Wasn't For Nothing - The Band JAREN
30. Highlands (Song of Ascent) - Benjamin William Hastings
31. Whole Heart (Hold Me Now) - Tayá, Aodhán King, Hillsong UNITED
32. Perfectly Loved - Rachael Lampa
33. Faith Is - Benjamin William Hastings

Bonus Track:
34. Homeward - Benjamin William Hastings

The link to this playlist can be found on my website.

about the author

Jessica Pietro has been enchanted by fantasy worlds her entire life. Though she dabbled in writing, she never anticipated being a published author.

In 2019, she began selling her artwork and teaching art under the name *Vellichor and More*. Then in 2021, after a horrible season of healing from past traumas, she began writing an epic fantasy series called *The Great King and the Seer*.

Two years later, she started *unfinished*. It took a while to get all of her thoughts out on paper, but she is at last ready for the world to see it.

Not only is Jessica passionate about art and stories, she also enjoys adventuring, boardgames, studying her bible, anime, music, hot tea, camping, and spending time with her family.

Jessica resides in Pennsylvania, with her husband, their son, and their kitties. Find out more about her by connecting with her on social media.

Links to all of her sites can be found here:
https://jessicapietroart.wixsite.com/1234/contact